Midnight Muse

Silvia Ardor

Midnight Muse © 2018 Silvia Ardor
Published 2018 by Belides Publishing Group
First Edition

ISBN 978-0-9976773-9-3

All images in this book are photographed by the author.

To following dreams.
To never settling.
To passion.
To you.

Contents

WHEN MIDNIGHT KNOCKS,
A MUSE AWAKENS...

Don't judge a book by its cover
Even as it sits propped open
Its pages screaming out at you
Don't look to the cover and squint your eyes
You might be surprised at what you will find
It might be collecting dust, crinkled, bent edges
Smells of musk
You may think you can see through the transparency
But learn to read between the lines
Words, pictures created in your mind
Please be kind and read cover to cover
For there are mysteries to unfold
Aimless whispers, secrets to be told
So entrust your eyes upon the ink, hold on tight
Bring it to your face and inhale with all your might
Breathe it in, feast your eyes on the raw
Passion that resides, so much to discover
So just please don't judge a book by its cover.

Midnight Muse

I've lost you again, Time.
I will never win this game of
hide
    and
        seek.

Time is an illusion
Like smoke rising from industrial plants
We believe that by trying to capture
its essence we may learn to control it.
But time laughs at our ignorance
It stands there, overpowering us
with the same calculating look it always
gives.
The evasive nature of it.
We become so weary by chasing it
Blindly grasping for the time when
all our will be's and one day's
knock us down, and we will swear
We'll gain forever, an eternity
if we only caught up to it.
But we are fools
Which is why time laughs
For we get older
Slowly, we whither
and take the fall
and time never existed at all.

Midnight Muse

It's cold outside love
Why don't you come, stay inside
Once out of hiding you'll feel the need
They'll charm you, and coax you, take you by the hand
Fill you with desire only to feed as planned
See a smile, looking for something real
A desolate place, from face to endless face
This is your playground but mind your step
They'll make you drip just for a single sip
Do you really want to be out in the cold love
But if you must go there's one thing you'll need
Take it with you, scatter it without greed
See it everywhere you go, with everyone you meet
Let it follow you around, even when you're beat
It's in the water, in the whispers of the leaves
It's the very air you breathe
So take this love
And let it hunt you down.

Come aboard our big white bus,
All you travelers are lost.
Leave behind things you hold dear;
Memories, Dreams, you won't need those here.

We have what will see you through
We'll gently suck the soul from you.
Don't you hold it wrapped so tight
We'll make everything alright.

Set aside your thoughts, the doubt
Your mind must clear, don't cry out.
This is the way, here is your cue
Say adieu to your point of view.

If you missed your chance this time
Listen to this internal rhyme
There is no need to ascertain,
We will find you.
We won't refrain; we'll surely be back again.

Midnight Muse

What darkness swirls inside your head?
You are the Pinot Noir beside my bed.

Midnight Muse

I'm stubborn. I say it straight.
I was raised well; kept my eyes open,
Even my ears.
Fought some battles, faced my fears.
But in all my years, I've never met
A man who could get me wet
From his dialogue, no regret.
Like sweat
In the summertime,
before the morning mildew's set.

Midnight Muse

Hey, you
Yes, you there flipping through
Sorry I'm straightforward but
I want you to do it.

Do it with your body
Do it with your hands
Do it with your lips
Or your fingers down my pants.

You can whisper,
You can swear
You can rip my underwear
Clench your fists,
Pull my hair
Take it all but please don't stare.

If you do it,
I want you raw
Follow your fucking dreams
And I'll take off my bra.

Filled with ecstasy
I've come undone, wind and sun
A day at the beach

Midnight Muse

It's like a love affair with Satan.
Your voice can permeate,
leave me paralyzed
Awaken a deep desire
A trancelike state,
where you penetrate
Lure me into an abysmal fire.

I was not alone
When thunder struck
Your silhouette flashed and chilled me to the bone
The unrelenting kiss of darkness
The flickering limelight, so weakened in despair
A mere shuddering spark before letting the night ensnare
With clenched fists at the haunting caress of summer breeze
Firm arms surround me, and I'm trapped
against the warmth of your hard chest
With a gasp I had to freeze, for
When thunder struck it didn't rest
I was hit with electric vibrations
Pushing against all I had suppressed
Sending sensations in waves, temptations
Pure pleasure, when into your eyes I gazed
What a complete surprise, to be struck by you
And be left certainly, undoubtedly, utterly amazed.

Midnight Muse

I saw a black cat walk right in front of me.
I smiled because he meowed, you see
I tripped and slid under a ladder,
No bruises anywhere; it doesn't matter.
I broke a mirror so I gasped
But with hair in my eyes I was masked
No "Jupiter Preserve You" when I sneeze
I'll keep my soul intact with just a squeeze
I killed a cricket, stepped on a crack
Birds no longer poop on my neck or back
If that doesn't make you shake your head,
I also woke up on the wrong side of the bed.

Midnight Muse

In the stillness surrounding me,
It eerily crept up so strong.
Scratching and burning at my throat
Suddenly couldn't feel more wrong

Another puff, I see the soft
Circular glow inside of me,
And with a flick I let my mind
Wander once more into the sea

I can't remember how to breathe,
But how can one expect to, when
Mimicking the mystical power
Only dragons knew back then

In silence I sit and ponder,
While my heartbeat quickens
Of its own volition, and
My breath shortens while the air thickens

Take back the memory, please rewind
Send me 10 minutes back in time
Can't stand the terror when I recall
That last damned cigarette of mine.

Midnight Muse

Will you burn me with desire?
I invite you to ignite my fire.
Come on darling, leave your mark
And consume me in the dark.

Midnight Muse

Make him wait

Appreciate

Anticipate

Reciprocate

Stir up his feelings

Concentrate, meditate.
Those words burn inside your blood
Breathe, like you know the meaning
And hush the noise that starts to flood.

There's no one but your eyes
Staring back at you
Demanding only diligence and strength
Take it all with no ado, dare you.

With every stretch, every pull
Every drop of sweat and moment met
Stay in control, keep your cool
Soon, you'll make them all drool.

Midnight Muse

It's the take-off that really gets you
That raw exhilaration in your breath
The butterflies in your breast
The feeling that you can go anywhere you desire to
When that desire starts pounding at your chest.

It tickles you with enticement
The brush of fingers, the stench of sex
Erotic fantasies explode out of confinement
Sensations so convoluted they perplex.

You're left gaping wide open, staggering
You're scared, you dare confess
Each whisper of spark on your skin, toying
Everything melting: inhibitions, stress.

Down the rabbit hole you keep falling
Though black as night you see so much
Closer, fogging up the glass between you
Pierced with ice; burned at the slightest touch.

Expecting solitude when you hit the ground
Until you're pinned up against the wall
And your soul is kissed tenderly, without a sound
By someone dark, handsome and tall.

Midnight Muse

I freeze in place, senses heightened
Out of time, out of space; I'm frightened.
I should just face
the cards I've been dealt
I went all in and you won the bet.

I'm cornered with nowhere to hide
You won't be denied, as I stare eyes wide.
You promised to take me
where promises don't last
I've fallen under the spell you've cast.

Midnight Muse

When I see you laughing with your big grin
You grasp my chin and begin
To extinguish the longing within
You ask where I've been
And I begin to tell you I was wearing thin
Because you are my safety pin
The healing resonance of a violin
A perfect synthesis of yang and yin
You make my head spin
Absolve all my sins
And leave me trembling with goose skin

Midnight Muse

If I'm just an ordinary girl
Who wishes for extraordinary love
If I remove my makeup
Natural like a cat, kind of
If I step towards you and inhale
Without cutting corners
Or trying to lure you with my tail
If I tell you about my life
And let the pieces fall where they may
If I reached out my arms
And opened the doors so you could lead the way
If I let go of fear
Close my eyes and lean over the edge
If I give you my trust
Knowing to you my life I'd pledge
If I sit with you in silence
And listen to the sound your mouth makes
If I laugh and cry and sing with you
Would you give me a chance for both our sakes
If I wait for you
Would you come back out of the blue
If I love you
Would you love me too?

Midnight Muse

Constrained by your
Deathly grip
My soul is
Yours.

Midnight Muse

I find myself fixated, on
You…asphyxiate me
Come now, show no mercy
I know you're thirsty

But I'm beyond your grasp
Oh my, that's my bra clasp
You'll surely make me sin
Hungry kisses on my skin

I told myself to never drown
Always smile and never frown
But you spike my kitty senses
And we drop all the pretenses

Not a word is spoken
You tear my world right open
Dig in deep and leave me faded
You have me fixated.

Midnight Muse

I long to be present in your presence.
Smothered by the thickness of your essence.
An energy so intoxicating from the start
Stirs an unspeakable desire in my heart.
I'll look at you, you'll look at me.
I feel your subtle authority.
What you need from me, I need from you, and I...
I wouldn't pursue it without you.
I'm entranced by you, and I would listen to you speak for hours.
Whether it be kneeling at your feet or on all fours.
Time will stop under your piercing gaze.
Oh, and the goosebumps you'll raise!
With your permission shall we start the ignition
If I grant you the key to my submission?

Midnight Muse

I could sell my soul to
the devil in your eyes.

Midnight Muse

You and she
After a few nights with her,
Then you come to me
I'm here for your pleasure, Monsieur.
You warm her bed and come back to me
You and she, so ordinary but is that what you need Sweet sir
When I know what feelings stir.
Another day with her and you come back to me
I'll give you my I's, she says, eyes penetrating gaze
As long as you keep coming back to me
Until the time that will inevitably reign
When you never stop coming to me again
And entangled darling we will be
You and she.

Midnight Muse

I have been so blind
I must've spaced out of my reality
These past long years but
You always pull me back you see
I shiver in your embrace while
I freeze and burn, ache and itch
You swallow me whole and I
gasp for air, in despair
but always hungry for more

I can't describe this yearning deep inside
It's like a part of me was meant to be
I wish I hadn't been so elusive with you
I know you must feel like I pushed you away
But the thing is, without you I'm lost
In my mind, my thoughts grow restless
A growing population, like bunnies
I get lost in there without you

So open up your pages, let me dance
and tickle you with the ink of dark romance.

The juices percolated from my lips,
at your fingertips.

Midnight Muse

Keep dancing this game with me
Surround my body with everlasting command
Please don't ever loosen your grip
The vibrations are sinking in, making me
Feel something again.
Use me as your tapestry, my every inch
Make me bleed the lust echoing in your eyes
Twist me, turn me, spin me upside down
Your expertise of the darkest thicket
of my mind
Awakens me and I can feel you
Drowning me with your liquid fire
I'll drink every last drop
I want this dance to never stop.

Midnight Muse

I want you to inhale me, impale me.
I want to boil under your touch.
I want to feel how much you crave me with every lap of your tongue.
I want to taste you, ensnare you.
I want your kiss to tear into my being and cease the beating of my heart.
I want your fire.
I want desire, passion, carnal; predator and prey.
I want to melt when our eyes lock.
I want you to fuck my mind.
I want your words to scar upon my bones and sear into my soul.
I want you to take control.
I want to be enslaved by you, submit myself to you, oh and bondage, too.
I want you inside me, but deeper.
I want nuclear fusion with you.

This silly game we play
Dancing around only to pound at our graves
Proceed with caution at every step like slaves
Don't step too soon but don't sit in the back
Learn to maneuver and slither which way

Lay back in wait for the time to spring to attack
Predator and prey, the cycle never betrays
For there is no sway that could keep the devil at bay
And the further you step you'll get lost in the depth
But you can't walk away so just hold your breath

These strings you entangle, the lies that you bled
Burrow into my head
But I hold the thread.

Midnight Muse

I feel the anger simmering beneath the surface
Knowing I put it there makes it hard to look you in the eyes
Just like the crumbled memories I can't erase
And the knots in my throat from our goodbyes

If only you could punish me for what I did
For what you made me do
But there's no escape, no matter where I hid
I wonder if you need it just as much as I do, too

To help release those dark feelings searing within
Since I will always be the one you blame
Won't you pick up your instrument and please begin
Bend me over at your whim and bring on the pain

Maybe this way we can move on
Maybe we can find closure
Maybe we'll carve a new path to walk upon
Or maybe we'll burn from the exposure

Midnight Muse

I tried chasing the sun
But time had already won.
Now I'm left panting, shaken
And the darkness time awakened
Seeks me out as if it knew
That my heart is frozen and blue.

Midnight Muse

When is the last time you got poked and prodded
When, just from the sight of it, your veins up and departed
Oh such sweet sorrow
when your internal temperature competes with the sun
When the heat flashes and the AC dashes and drones out the
silence with its bellowing sound
And you turn it off but you can't even enjoy a cigarette on the
patio
And the radio doesn't play any good music anymore, no
It's cold
When's the last time you donned a wool jacked in July
Would you be so bold as to combat the chill brewing up inside
Oh but it's almost as if you couldn't see
Watery eyes, blurry vision; the devil on a maniacal mission
Busy is as busy goes and a sneeze here and you reach for it, but
All the tissues are gone.
So you drag yourself to bed by your nose and curl up your toes
Beg for mercy and hope come the morrow you'll feel better, so
Off you doze.
Eyes closed.

Midnight Muse

While I try so hard to fall asleep
You penetrate my thoughts deep
I'm standing on the ledge, steep
I ask myself should I take the leap
Yet I'm back to counting sheep
I feel like Little Bo Peep
When I think I've forgotten you, creep
My heart starts to skip a beep
But I'm blinded by the upkeep
It's me you'll objectify to keep
Off my feet you intend to sweep
Like I couldn't give a bleep
No matter how deep your fingers seep
What you sow is what you reap
Eyes slide shut, unable to weep
Fade into a paradoxical sleep

Midnight Muse

It's lonely in here
Rummaging through thoughts
But not as lonely as I was with you by my side
You changed your mind
Not sure of yourself
You were magnificent
Tragically blind
You turned away from my open mind
The silence between us grew darker and thick
You know toxic adhesives never stick
I won't be removed
From my self respect
I know someone will come for me and make me forget
Who will leave me alone in my tangled web
Imperturbably serene
I'll be his main cuisine
He'll wrap me in his arms so closely
I will never again be
Lonely

A meandering leaf in the rainforest
I am that, and nothing more.

A crystal fragment in a dazzling geode
I am that, and nothing more.

A shooting star during a meteor shower
I am that, and nothing more.

A black hole in the infinite universe
I am that, and nothing more.

A cool bracing dip beneath a waterfall
You are that, and nothing more.

Midnight Muse

In the past when we would dine
You would render me asinine

Couldn't help but undermine
You wanted me as your concubine
To carry on your bloodline
You can't be mine.

Our blood will never learn to clot
More often than not
Your alkaline sensibilities
Will not fail to shine.

So with red wine, I am divine
While you, distraught
An afterthought.

Midnight Muse

And through it all; the one word answers
Which thoroughly revealed

I threw caution to the wind
Just to ride through the park with you

And every glance you threw
I couldn't see through you

You threw me away
And I was through with you

The trees have eyes
What a surprise
As if from evolution
They've come into fruition
Shrouded in silence
Witnessing violence
What would you see
If you were a tree?

Midnight Muse

I can't stand this whirring in my mind
Being stung by bees is one of my greatest fears
I should've written,
all these years
When instead I'd burst in tears.

Now I'm lost, I can't find
Words jumbled, crumpled up
in towers of scattered files
of feelings.
I had become numb to the
aching in my breast;
not a tear since then, I must attest.

A two-faced path to freedom
The soothing summer air caressing me
how light and surreal;
While icy waves crash against
my inner being, what an ordeal
Slowly close my eyes and kneel.

I shudder from the aftershock
of opening my door a crack.
Just a peek, I feel it pour out of me,
everything I see.
Like a bubbling spring, or a bumblebee.

So I write
To face my fears,
get the buzzing out of my ears.

Miss you, I do not
    But I don't miss
a lot.

Midnight Muse

To be in solitude is
Figures running inside my head
To test the time I've spent in bed
To feel like it will never end

To basking in the present moment
Lone thoughts whispering in my ear
To be a shaky breath from fear
To fight for what you and I hold dear

To the laughs we've shared, and time
Though time flees so suddenly
To still choose me hungrily
To admit you're ready

To wanting it to never end
Finding peace in your embrace
To your warm hands upon my face
To the day I hope you'll call

To go all in like you've said
And face the struggle and the cold
To together never getting old
To be loved and
To love

Midnight Muse

You bind me, unwind me
And yet
I yearn for more, of
You.

In time and time and time again
I look back at my life
Leaning back a bit too far
I could almost feel the knife

And life will sell you pretty lies
But there's no perfect fit
I could stretch and bend and fold and squeeze
But I'm no match for your wit

You pass me by while I stand still
Sleep, yoga, work, eat
The days will come and there they go
I have you on repeat

My life will be the price I pay
When you lure me with your smile
I can't tell what's real or not
Come, won't you stay a while

Midnight Muse

It starts to crawl up from my toes
Like the BP oil spill, it spreads
All over me
It seeps inside
I'm paralyzed
It freezes
Numbs
Can't feel my...
I quiver, shake
Precipitate
My heart shatters
In an infinite loop
I should retreat
Subside. But,
I hears there are molten lava pools
Fields of golden fire on the other side.

Midnight Muse

My person is out there...
He's just stuck in traffic:
Fifth Element status.

Midnight Muse

I sometimes meet up with my soulmate in my dreams.
Those moments, well some of them are quite heated.
Fantasies come to life.
He knows just what to do to creep under my skin
The time I get to spend with this faceless master
of my heart
is infinite, crammed in those few nights,
few fragments, in my mind.
Sometimes he even makes me forget he was ever there.
But I always know it's him when his energy materializes within me.
I hope he pays me a visit tonight.
I hope he finds his way into my life.
I'll be here.

What is love, but the ability
To be in the same comfortable,
Intimate space
Together and behold each other
In the eyes.
It's not just looking at your eyes, but
Letting the world
Crumble
And seeing you as you really are:
Magnificent, mesmerizing and
Incredibly naked.

Midnight Muse

My heart has a quality
It loves to fall in love you see
It can get quite weary
Dreary; all the possibilities
But there's only one with the capability
His ability
To feel my desires, read me
Quite possibly his voice
Would leave me no choice
To get lost in his eyes
No hiding behind alibis
He'd make me surrender
Leave me breathless, his tender
Touch; his whispers in my ear
Would make my fear disappear
But until he is near
I'll wait patiently
And keep my fragile heart
Beating passionately
Under lock and key

Midnight Muse

The universe is whispering to me.
It feels familiar, as if this has happened before.
The grand voice resonates throughout my entire
body and leaves my limbs weeping in sweet torture.
I can feel the beat of my heart vibrating out of every pressure
point.
I close my eyes to let the feeling consume me and
so I could quiet my mind and listen,
"Your soul is singing to me of happiness.
Keep yourself happy and remember to love yourself always."
Why do I have the feeling I won't remember
any of this in the morning?
I won't forget
I won't, for
I won't
I.

We vibrate on this frequency
Side by side, unified
Parallel to each other.
But sometimes we get too close
Back to back, we're intertwined.
And at the slightest touch
We're pulled in tight, then far apart.
And we feel that electric shock
That makes us miss each other.
Skip days, weeks, months
Until eventually, inevitably
We find ourselves back together.
The calm after the storm, this time
On that same frequency.

Midnight Muse

So she ran away, to a cabin nestled deep in the canyons of a ranch
somewhere off the beaten path.
Four books in her possession; each so different,
but the culmination a labyrinth into her being.
One for the mind, one for the hunger in her heart, and two for the
soul.
You can never have enough books for the soul.

On the open road.
Where it leads will I ever know?
Running from the noise, my fears…
will they follow me?
Along this winding road towards my sanctuary.
Where nature whispers
and the Yuba flows in wait,
And the silence finds me at half past eight.

With pillows galore
Cats chasing on the floor.
Whispers of dreams
With vehement screams.
I sink into clouds, snuggle in tight
Dive into my mind and bid you good night.

ABOUT THE AUTHOR

Silvia Ardor is a writer based in Los Angeles, CA. She is originally from Bucharest, Romania. She penned the name "Ardor", which means passion, fervor, fire, verve, to stand for the type of writing and expression she exudes.

She finds that new ideas and rhymes start flowing while driving home from work or during her Bikram yoga classes. Silvia actively practices meditation in various forms, some of which include long drives and seven hour baking sessions. She is excited to see where this passion for writing will take her.

Follow her on Instagram for new poetry, original quotes, and upcoming releases. @silvia.ardor